Write a Conference Proposal the Conference Wants and Accepts

Johanna Rothman

Write a Conference Proposal the Conference Wants and Accepts

Johanna Rothman

ISBN 978-1-943487-22-6

Practical **ink**

Contents

Acknowledgements

I could not have written this book without having read hundreds of proposals. Thank you, proposal writers, for having the courage to write your proposal and for allowing me to read them.

I also thank all the people who've offered me feedback about my proposals. You helped me craft better proposals and help other people see my work.

I thank Nancy Swaine for copyediting.

Cover by Brandon Swann, swanndesignstudio.com

All mistakes are mine.

Cover photo by Matt Botsford on Unsplash

1. Prepare to Present at a Conference

You want to present a talk, workshop, or an experience report at a conference. (Or, a lightning talk, Pecha Kucha, or more.) You have something important to share. How can you create a proposal that the program committee will accept?

You write a proposal.

I've been a professional speaker to support my consulting business for 25 years. I've delivered several hundred presentations of some variety: track talks, workshops, keynotes, lightning talks, Pecha Kuchas, and panel presentations.

I've had to write a proposal for each of them.

And I've been a reviewer, a track chair, and an experience report shepherd for the Agile 20xx series of conferences for more than 10 years. I've also been an experience report shepherd for the XP 20xx conferences for several years.

I've had to read too many horrible proposals.

I'm happy to share what I've learned in this book. As you work through the proposal writing, do let me know if you have questions or comments.

I make no claims that the ideas here are the One Right Way to create a conference proposal. I've developed these ideas over the years, refining what works for me.

Some of these ideas will work for you. I hope all of them will, but you may have to adapt them to your circumstances.

My best wishes and I hope the conferences accept your well-crafted, honed proposals.

Let's start.

2. Frame the Proposal

You might think you just "start at the top" and write a conference proposal. I have found that thinking about the proposal a little differently helps me create a *better* proposal. I start with a *frame*, something that my proposal readers might not see at all. That helps me set the context and create a great proposal.

Consider these steps to a conference proposal:

1. Frame the proposal: Understand who and what purpose the proposal serves.
2. Understand the five parts of the proposal: title, abstract, description, learning outcomes, and your bio.
3. Iterate on the proposal parts and strengthen your writing as you iterate.
4. Decide which conference(s) to submit your proposal.
5. Obtain the most timely feedback from your proposal.

I can't guarantee a conference will accept your proposal if you follow these steps. However, my acceptance rate climbed significantly when I started to think about conference proposals this way.

That's because you can create a proposal the program committee wants to accept.

2.1 Sell Your Session with Your Proposal

A conference proposal serves these purposes:

- Help the conference program committee select your proposal.
- Help the people at the conference select your session.

That business of selection means your proposal has to invite people to connect with your ideas.

These ideas help me frame that connection:

- Who do I want to connect with?
- What problems do these people have?
- Is there a specific context I want to address?

Your session has solutions that are not right for everyone. Your experience has a context, and that context matters. The context often helps me select who I want to connect with.

2.1.1 Who Is Your Audience?

When you choose your audience, you start to clarify what you might want to say and how to frame your work.

Your proposal is the first way you connect with your audience.

For example, I only offer talks for people using agile approaches or trying to. Why? Because I restrict my consulting work to people who want to use agile approaches. (I also work in an agile way.)

I respect people who don't want to use agile approaches. However, I am not interested in consulting in their context. I'm happy to discuss their issues over a cup of coffee. Not for work.

What if you're *not* a consultant? It's the same problem. Who do *you* want to connect with?

Beware of selecting a large class of people, such as "Scrum Masters," "agile coaches," or even "managers." Yes, there are many of those people.

Because there are many of those people, they have many problems. Lots of people means lots of problems. And, they often need different answers depending on their context.

All of those contexts means you are unlikely to help *all* of those people in one session.

It's okay to start with a large class of people. Make sure you narrow your focus when you identify the problems those people have. (I'll talk more about this later.)

2.1.2 Identify Your Audience's Problems

In a session at Agile 2019 about how to write a conference proposal, I sat next to a lovely guy who said he wanted to give a talk about helping teams be happy.

I asked why he wanted teams to be happy. I find that happiness is an outcome of being satisfied with the work, not a direct goal itself. He looked at me with astonishment. He said, "Don't all teams need to be happy?"

I said, "No, not at all. Team members need to be satisfied with and proud of their work. You can't control a person's happiness, especially not at work."

"Ooooh."

I'm not sure what he thought after that.

I am sure that his thesis—that teams need to be happy—is a response to problems he observed at work. That happiness response might have worked for him. But what matters *more* to the conference (and the audience) are the *problems* he observed.

Think back to the people you identified as the people you want in your audience. Use their problems to connect with them.

What problems does your potential audience—the people you want to connect with—have?

2.1.3 Beware of Making People Feel Stupid or Wrong

People work in a particular context. You might think they have their problems for stupid reasons. You might even think they are wrong.

Remember, their context almost always drives their decision-making. You might think they make wrong decisions. They think that what they do makes total sense in their context.

I have a great talk called (right now) "Learn to Say No and Manage Your Multitasking!" I love giving that talk. And, when I propose it, I don't tell people they are wrong for either multitasking or requesting multitasking.

I first bring people along with a story, and then I explain how people are mistaken in their beliefs. Here's how I often start that talk:

Start With a Story

Back when I was a young developer, my boss asked me to work 50% on Project A, 35% on Project B, and 15% on Project C. I looked at him, and asked, "In my copious free time, should I also work on Projects D and E?"

He said, "Oh, yes, please do."

That's what I mean by a story. Most of us have either heard those kind of requests, or made those requests. I use this as a story to connect with people.

I know multitasking is wrong. I also know that well-meaning people might not know what I know. They certainly have trouble saying no to their bosses. That's why I propose the talk.

I stay empathetic to their problems:

- These people multitask.
- They might or might not know multitasking is "wrong."
- Their real problem is they have no idea how to stop multitasking.

I meet people where they are, starting in the proposal. That's part of connecting with people about their problems.

2.1.4 Define the Context

I already said I only speak to people who are on their agile journey or experimenting with that journey. That's my context for my talks.

You will choose your context.

You might choose a product domain, such as financial products. You might select a specific function, such as testers. You
might select a company size.

Those are just three possibilities. You have many options for
the context.

Your suggestions are not right for all possible people. If you
don't know when your solutions don't work, you might not
realize what the problem is or what the answers are. When
you tell people how or when your solutions don't work, you
build your authority. (Brian Marick taught me that trick many
years ago when he was a technical editor for a magazine.)

Don't be afraid of narrowing your context. People are smart.
Even when I specifically say "project or program managers"
in my abstract, some developers and testers come to my talks.
Why? Because they have the same problems I wrote about in
my proposal. And, they are willing to look past the context I
set to explore their problems.

2.2 Start Your Proposal

Create your proposal document in the editor of your choice.
I recommend you keep all the pieces of your proposal in
one document. When you keep everything together, you can
create your submission for the conference easily.

Start with your frame for the proposal:

1. Who is your audience? Who do you want to come to
   your session?

2. What problems do they have? List them in some way. If you can't write down at least three problems, you might not understand this particular topic enough. That's okay—you might select one type of presentation over another. For example, you might decide to facilitate an exploratory workshop to explore the problems people see.
3. What is the context? A great proposal will also describe when your solutions *don't* work. That's why the best proposals set the context.

Now that you understand who you want to connect with, the problems they have, and the context, we'll address the outcomes you want to achieve.

3. Start with Outcomes

Now that you've framed your proposal, start with what you want people to learn from your session, the outcomes.

Why? Because too many descriptions are a promise for an outcome or what people will learn. If you're coy about the outcomes, people can't select themselves in or out for your presentation.

Do not kid yourself and say, "Everyone should hear my ideas." Your content is not right for everyone. (Mine isn't either.)

You are better off speaking to/with five interested people than to 500 people who could not care less about your topic. You don't need a lot of people to use and spread your ideas. You only need people who are passionate about your topic to apply and spread your ideas.

Help people become interested in your topic with outcomes—the value they receive from your session.

3.1 Outcomes Start with Verbs

Think about a conference presentation you enjoyed. What did you like about it? You might have liked the various ways the speaker helped you to:

- Remember: An easy way to remember the facts.

- Understand: How to understand a concept. You might not have known about the idea before. Even if you had known, maybe this time, you gained more insight.
- Apply: How to apply this new information to your situation.
- Analyze: How to connect the ideas to your context. Maybe even how to create an experiment to use the ideas.
- Evaluate: Appraise your decisions or make new ones.
- Create: You gained an "aha" moment where you can now use these ideas to create your own ideas.

These words are from Bloom's Taxonomy. I'm not showing the pyramid, because I don't buy the pyramid. Supposedly the things first on my list are less "useful." However, I don't know how to create, evaluate, analyze, or apply without remembering and understanding.

Here's the problem with a proposal: People learn by doing. People make connections to your content in ways you can't predict.

Here are two things that have been true for me in my 25 years as a professional speaker:

- I can't depend on anyone evaluating my session for the conference to understand what I mean.
- I can't rely on any participant understanding what I mean.

I often need to flow "up" and "down" Bloom's Taxonomy so I can share my ideas well.

That's why I start with verbs.

3.2 See Examples of Outcomes

In my multitasking talk, I offer these outcomes:

- See the problems of multitasking, including the costs to a person, the team, and the organization.
- Experiment with ways to expose all the work.
- Analyze your situation.
- Practice saying No.

Depending on how much time I have for that presentation, I either use a simulation or a conversation for the "Practice saying No" outcome.

Yes, I did capitalize the No. That's because people have trouble saying No. I use capitalization to emphasize the No.

Let's go a little meta and discuss each of these:

1. See the problems including costs, means I will explain how to identify the multitasking and assess how much time people waste.
2. Experiment with ways to expose the work means I will offer several possibilities to visualize and discuss the work.
3. Analyze your situation is about connecting the participant with the ideas. As with many ideas, everyone's context is different.
4. Practice saying No means people will use their mouths.

Your proposal will have different outcomes. However, do you see how the outcomes might drive your abstract/description? Outcomes also help you select a great title.

3.3 Hook the Reader with Actionable Outcomes

Remember in the previous chapter, Frame the Proposal, how you identified your audience's problems? (See Identify Your Audience's Problems.) Now, you'll see how the outcomes you offer will fix their problems. (Maybe not fix, but offer these people a starting point to address their problems.)

Consider how you will hook your reader with actionable outcomes:

1. Start each outcome with a verb so people can imagine themselves doing this very thing. That's why I like to start with verbs.
2. Share your secrets or tips in the proposal. Do not promise an outcome, as in "Johanna will share the secrets of avoiding multitasking." No! Explain those secrets in the proposal.
3. Vary the verbs as much as you can and still keep the sentences reasonable. I often start with "See this" or "See that." After the 5th time I've written "See," I realize I'm talking about other verbs. Vary the actions you want people to take at the end of the session.

Do you know specific terms of art that other people might think are jargon? Beware of adding those terms.

For example, I did not discuss the Cost of Delay (CoD) in the outcomes. CoD is not jargon, but it might sound that way to people. I might add CoD later, depending on what I write for the abstract. However, too few people still know about CoD.

As I iterate over the entire proposal, I'll decide whether to add it in later.

(For more information about Cost of Delay, see *Diving for Hidden Treasures: Uncovering the Cost of Delay Your Project Portfolio.*)

And, some conferences are so impressed with themselves that they love jargon. I tend not to propose anything for those conferences.

However, you might need to play the conference game. Decide how you will frame your outcomes. I tend to err on the side of simplicity so that people can say yes to my proposal.

3.4 Add to Your Proposal

Update your proposal document with this information:

1. Review the people you want to participate in or attend your presentation. What do you want them to learn/realize/engage in some way from your session? List the outcomes. I try to have four or five outcomes. That's a guideline, not a rule.
2. Start the outcomes with verbs. I don't happen to like, "You will learn" as a start. I know I'm going to learn something. Please, get to the point with a verb.
3. How well do the outcomes match the list of problems you developed in Identify Your Audience's Problems? Sometimes, when I start a proposal, I realize I have lumped several problems in one proposal. I need to create two proposals. The outcomes help me separate the various problems and create the necessary proposals.

Next, we'll talk about the abstract, that first paragraph that
people read.

4. Create Your Abstract

You've decided who your session is for: people with specific problems. You've got the outcomes, the value the people with problems will receive from your session. Now, it's time to write the abstract.

Conference proposals always have a short abstract. Some conferences, such as the Agile 20xx conferences, also have "Information for the Program Team." You might think of that as the outline or more information about what you're proposing. I'll address that later.

4.1 Hook People with Your Abstract

When *you* go to conferences, what makes *you* consider a session?

- The speaker: You've heard this speaker before, or the speaker is famous in some way.
- The title: Something about the title grabbed you, connected with you.
- The abstract/short description: The first paragraph that explains *your* problems, and offers you some possibilities.

Any of those might be what hooks the eventual attendee. To get to the conference, you need to hook the program committee.

Help the program committee accept your session based on your abstract.

4.2 Write First For the Program Committee

You might think the people going to the conference are your audience. They are, and they are the *second* audience.

Your first audience is the program committee. The program committee consists of all the gatekeepers for the conference. The gatekeepers include:

- Track chairs
- Track reviewers
- Anyone else who can reject your session.

Here are my assumptions about the program committee:

- They want the conference to be a big success.
- They care that people will learn something new or learn how to make an "old" idea work better.
- They might or might not care about *you*. They care about the success of the conference.

That means your abstract has to influence the program committee so they will choose you.

4.3 Write a Succinct Abstract

I've been a reviewer for many conferences. Too often, I read rambling "abstracts"—four, five, or six paragraphs of confusing-to-me language. Not only does the language confuse me, but I also can't tell what I'm going to learn from the abstract.

I use two primary approaches:

- Kent Beck's One Startling Sentence
- Hey! You! See? So...

If you read my blog posts, you see that I use One Startling Sentence (OSS) a lot. OSS helps me set the context for the reader. That means I also use OSS for articles and short book descriptions. I often use OSS to set the context in longer form, such as for a chapter in a book.

4.3.1 Consider One Startling Sentence

I no longer remember how or when I discovered Kent Beck's *One Startling Sentence,* but I am thrilled I did.

One Startling Sentence consists of a four-sentence paragraph in this order:

- First sentence: What's the problem?
- Second sentence: Why is this problem a problem?
- Third sentence: Startling sentence.
- Fourth sentence: Implication of the startling sentence.

Here's the first-draft example for my multitasking talk:

1. You're working on so many projects, you can't tell what
   to do first.
2. Multitasking is the fastest way to stop a project in its
   tracks. Even worse, people feel hopeless about their
   work.
3. You can say *No* or *When?*—especially when you visualize your work and discuss your options with the powers-
   that-be.
4. You'll finish more projects, have more pride in your
   work, and everyone's throughput will increase.

As a first draft, that's not bad.

Yes, I have two sentences for the second sentence. That's
because there are problems pervade the organization, the
project, and the person. I don't yet know how to make this one
sentence. I hope that people identify with either the project
problems or the person problems. If I'm lucky, they'll connect
with both sets of problems.

You might wonder—can't I use the abstract from the last time
I gave this talk? I could. I choose not to until I get to the point
where I think I can't improve on the abstract.

Yes, I iterate over my abstracts until I can no longer improve
them.

I changed the abstract every time I proposed this talk. The
slides don't change that much. However, I often rework the
abstract to make the abstract more inviting.

And, sometimes, especially if I'm an invited speaker, conferences want just a title. I get lazy and don't write or update
the abstract. Until it's time to send in the proposal to the
conference. That's when I update the abstract.

Sometimes, One Startling Sentence isn't quite right. That's when I use "Hey! You! See? So..."

4.3.2 Consider Hey! You! See? So...

I also don't remember when I learned this approach to an opening. A colleague whose writing I enjoyed explained it to me. He had learned it earlier—possibly from Gerald M. Weinberg.

Hey! grabs the reader's attention. It can be an entire sentence or a fragment of an idea. And, the readers need to see it within the first couple of sentences, so the reader will continue reading.

You! means how does this idea affect the reader? What about this writing makes it relevant to the reader?

See? is the example piece, the part where the author helps the reader see what the author is talking about.

So... is what you want the reader to do about this once he or she is done reading the work.

Remember, back in Frame the Proposal, you made a list of the people you want to attract and the problems they have? That's what the Hey and You parts are.

Here's an example for the multitasking proposal:

1. Are you a project manager, Scrum Master, or agile coach, attempting to support, lead, or serve multiple projects or teams?
2. Do you feel pulled in so many directions you feel as if you can't make any progress?

3. If so, you can learn to manage your personal project portfolio.
4. You'll see how to show your boss(es) all the work you're supposed to do, and how to have the tough "No" conversation.

This is another four-sentence paragraph. It works as an abstract.

4.4 Write a One-Paragraph Abstract

For abstracts, shorter is better. Use one short paragraph for your abstract.

You don't have to use One Startling Sentence or Hey! You! See! So... You might select a different approach to your abstracts. Your approach doesn't matter. Only write one short paragraph for your abstract.

Do you have more to say? Most conferences ask for a longer description later on in the proposal. Keep your abstract to one paragraph.

Remember these points:

- Connect with your reader. Your first reader is the program committee.
- Lead with problems. Offer specifics so the program committee can see you have substance behind your proposal.
- Make the end of the paragraph as upbeat as you can make it. (That's the primary outcome for the audience, what people will learn.)

If you really have more to say and you think it belongs in the abstract, test your ideas.

4.5 Test Your Abstract

A colleague told me he needed four paragraphs to fully define his abstract. He wrote four paragraphs, each using the One Startling Sentence approach.

- The first paragraph discussed the need for test automation.
- The second paragraph discussed the time teams need to build their test automation.
- The third paragraph discussed the need to be able to reset the environment for test automation.
- The fourth paragraph discussed how to make the test results self-explanatory.

When I told him he had four proposals, he didn't believe me. I suggested he Start with Outcomes. He learned he had four proposals. And, each proposal spoke to a different audience.

Here's how you might test your abstract:

1. Who are the people who need to hear your information, just based on the first paragraph in your abstract?
2. Are they the same people you identified in Who Is Your Audience? Do you have fewer or more people? Fewer people isn't a problem. More people might mean you haven't focused your abstract.
3. Is there something in the abstract that is unique? Or, at least, not something obvious?

You might have other criteria for your abstract. I find when I test my abstracts, I make them more useful to everyone. (And, more interesting for me.)

4.6 Support the Abstract with More Information

Sometimes, I add more paragraphs to my abstract to support the first paragraph. Some program committees, such as the committees for the Agile 20xx or the PMI conferences, like to read more in an abstract. They want more information because they receive so many proposals.

I have noticed something important. The audience for these additional words is rarely the conference audience. The audience is almost always the program committee.

I could be cynical and say they are looking for reasons to reject your proposal. I don't actually think they're looking to reject. However, the program committee looks for the *most* valuable content. This is your chance to show how valuable your content can be.

You might want to add more detail, so you can show your authority and knowledge of the topic.

When I add more paragraphs, I start with the problems and add more information. Here is a way I might add supporting material, after that first paragraph:

> Multitasking pervades every organization. Unless you measure the costs of multitasking, including cycle time, you might not realize how much trying

to do "everything" costs a person, a team, and the organization.

You can measure those costs in several ways: creating a value stream map, calculating Cost of Delay, and measuring a team's cycle time.

Even better, if you create a board—and I'll show examples of simple boards—you can create transparency for the problem. Since not everyone believes the cost calculations, you might have better luck with boards.

Armed with data, you can have discussions about what to continue, what to stop for now, and what to do *never*. You don't need a career-limiting-conversation. You can have a conversation and create win-win outcomes for you, the project, and the organization.

Here's what I did in these paragraphs:

- Alluded to more outcomes, such as the costs of multitasking, how to measure those costs, and examples of boards and conversations.
- Clarified the problems.
- Clarified what I will say.

I help the program committee believe I will do a great job with this additional information.

Now, I can assess my outcomes and see if I want to change them. I often do.

4.7 Update Your Outcomes

My previous outcomes were:

- See the problems of multitasking, including the costs to a person, team, and the organization.
- Experiment with ways to expose all the work.
- Analyze your situation.
- Practice saying No.

Based on my changes, I can add these outcomes:

- Show at least three ways of calculating the costs of multitasking for a person, a team, and the organization.
- Explain how to create a board that reflects multitasking.
- Prepare for the conversation so you and your boss can agree on what to finish now, what to work on later, and what to never do.

I iterate over the outcomes as much as I iterate over the abstract.

4.8 Separate the Writing from the Editing

When I teach writing, I teach people to separate the writing from the editing. That means:

- Write your abstract as one paragraph of four sentences. (Five, if you must.) I actually write the four sentences separately, as I showed you above.

- *After* you have all the sentences, check them with the grammar checker of your choice. Check for readability and passive voice.
- Excise passive voice. I don't care how many words it takes you, make sure there is *no* passive voice in an abstract.
- Check your readability and grade levels. The higher the readability score, the better. A readability score of 65 or higher is good. A grade level of less than Grade 8 is good.

I try to keep my readability over 65 and my grade level close to 6. Yes, I realize everyone reading conference submissions is smart, probably has a degree or equivalent, and has substantive worked experience. I work on readability to make sure I invite them into my writing. Why make the program committee work hard at reading what I wrote?

Remember, the program committee has hundreds of proposals to read. Make your proposal easy to read and they are more likely to accept your proposal.

Iterate on your abstract until you have four sentences with no passive voice, a readability score over 60, and a grade level of about Grade 6.

When I checked the readability of my abstract, Word gave it a readability score of 70 and a grade level of 6.7. Grammarly gave it a readability score of 75 and a grade level of 7. That's good enough, at least for now.

4.9 Add Your Abstract and Update Your Proposal

Open your proposal document. As you update your proposal with your abstract, also iterate over the outcomes and the people you want to attract to your session.

1. Write your abstract. I recommend One Startling Sentence, but you might choose an alternative. Regardless of how you organize, start the abstract with the problems you see that your session will address.
2. How long is that paragraph? If the abstract is more than five sentences, what can you do to shorten the paragraph to four or five sentences? You might need supporting paragraphs.
3. Check the readability of your abstract. Can you make it more readable? A lower grade level? You can't always simplify, but I find it's worth trying. Remember, an easy-to-read abstract attracts readers and the right audience.

Now that you have your abstract, it's time to finish the rest of the description.

5. Complete the Proposal

You know who your audience is because you framed the proposal. You created your initial outcomes, and you refined those outcomes when you wrote the abstract.

Now it's time to complete the rest of the proposal, excluding your bio and the title. Bios and titles are different from the rest of the proposal.

Every conference proposal seems to be a little different. Depending upon the venue and the organizer, every conference proposal will be a little different. But the one part every conference requests is a description of the *type* of session.

5.1 Define Your Session Type

Here are the session types I know about.

- Talk or presentation. You might lead interactions, but it's not a workshop. The audience expects you to wow them with your ideas and insights.
- Workshop. When people see the word, "workshop," they expect to work, not just listen to you talk. The audience expects to work through some problem or other, and gain their own personal insights.

- Experience report. You tell the story of some significant change, often in an organization. The audience expects a *story*, where they can learn from your insights.
- Lightning talk. A reduced-time presentation, such as 5 or 10 minutes. No one expects you to lead any interactions. The audience expects one important idea—that yes, offers them insights.
- Pecha Kucha. A specific form of a presentation: 20 slides, each in 20 seconds. A total of 6:40 minutes. The slides are supposed to be pictures. The audience might not know what to expect if they have never seen a Pecha Kucha before. Your job is to entertain, often with a little inspiration. You don't interact in the session.
- Panel. A panel is a limited number of people who will take various stances on the questions at hand. I don't propose panels. I love participating, but I don't propose them.

Each session type offers you and the potential audience something a little different.

5.2 Choose Your Session Type

Not all conferences want all possible session types. In my experience, you most often choose between a talk, workshop, and an experience report. However, many conferences offer the opportunity for lightning talks and Pecha Kuchas once they accept your main presentation.

I ask myself these questions, to decide which session type I want to offer:

- Is this *one* specific experience where I can discuss a change? I'll choose the experience report.
- Do I have several experiences that I can mine for common, useful ideas? I'll choose a presentation or talk.
- Do I have enough time to mine those common ideas and create a workshop so people can practice? I'll choose a workshop.

The session type might also depend on the time for each session.

Here's my problem. When I create a workshop, people learn as they try something new. And, just the trying isn't sufficient. I need to lead a debrief of their experience to help them understand and integrate what they learned.

I have had reasonable results in a 60-minute workshop with one interaction and one debrief. I often feel as if I "should" have been able to do more.

I prefer to offer a presentation with some short interactions. I don't have to fully debrief if I only have one hour.

With 75 or 90 minutes, I prefer to offer a workshop. That duration allows me the opportunity to craft two or three interactions and debrief them.

Note: Some conferences create an expectation that *attendees* only have to open their eyes and ears and us speakers can pour great information into their heads. That's why the conference calls the people who attend "attendees." The program committee doesn't call those people "participants."

Too often, in the really big conferences, these attendees expect a recipe. That's because they have so many interconnected problems, the people find it difficult to unlink the various problems from each other. When people expect a recipe, they don't consider how to adapt your ideas to their circumstances.

I don't know what to suggest. I urge you to recognize this phenomenon and to build as many interactions as possible into your session. The more interactions, the more people realize they will need to adapt what you say to their circumstances.

Before you create a title, finish the rest of the proposal.

5.3 Complete the Other Parts of the Proposal

Many conferences now ask speakers to offer an outline of what they will say. In the Agile 20xx conferences, that section is called "Information for the Program Committee" or some such wording like that.

"More information" offers you a chance to show the program committee you *know your topic*. The audience will be in your capable hands. If there is a place for more information, fill this in. Otherwise, the program committee can't easily say yes to your proposal. Your job is to help these people say yes.

This extra information is a little different for a talk/workshop than it is for an experience report.

One formatting note: Make sure you explain this information in relatively short paragraphs. Check the grade level and readability of this text, also. Don't make people work hard to read your information.

5.3.1 Information for a Talk or Workshop

I fill in the Information box with an outline of what I think I'm going to say, in five-minute increments.

I start with the context, often in the form of a short story. This shows the program committee who the session is for, and the problem they have.

For the multitasking talk, I often start with this:

> 0:00-0:05 mins: Tell the story of when I was a young engineer and my boss wanted me to work on 3 projects.

This is why I like to start with the proposal frame. I know who I want in my audience. I know their problems. I'll still have to help the program committee see my solutions, but they can see I'm inviting people into the material and connecting with these people right away.

As a reviewer, when I read something like this, I relax a little. I'm pretty sure the writer knows what they're talking about.

Your opening sets the context for the audience.

Avoid These Three Common Problems When Starting a Talk

Never start a talk with how happy you are to be here. We know you're happy.

Never start a talk with information about your company—unless it's an experience report and you think you need to start the talk that way. I would still start it with,

> "How many of you have ever been in this situation?" and
> itemize the problems. Never start with how large/small
> your company is and how much revenue you had. If that
> information is relevant, add it *after* your opening story.
>
> Never start a talk with your introduction. "I've been
> an agile coach for 5 years"—unless that information is
> relevant to the problems your audience has. No one cares
> where you work, how long you've worked. They have
> problems. They want answers, or at the very least, an idea
> they can apply to their situation.

Start the talk with a way to connect to the people you want
in your audience and their problems.

In my experience, the larger the conference, the more detail
the program committee wants. That's why I explain the
outline in 5-minute increments.

When I write the talk, I often change the order of the information for better flow. I keep the story at the front, but I change
how the rest of the session goes. If you also do that, make sure
you deliver on the outcomes you described.

For a workshop, I describe the interaction in words similar to
this:

> "From the worksheet, work in triads discussing
> the specific points above. Debrief what people dis-
> cussed and wrote down."

I often use 10-15 minutes for this kind of interaction.

For the simulation I use in the multitasking talk, I might use
these words:

"Encourage people to try the various words. Debrief. Timebox this total activity to 7 minutes."

When the program committee sees explanations like this, they know I know what I'm planning to do.

I don't actually create or update the talk or the workshop until a couple of months in advance of the conference. That's because the call for submissions opens quite early, and often closes more than six months in advance of the conference.

However, I have a zeroth design for every interaction. And, because I offer a reasonable outline for the talk or workshop, the program committee believes I will deliver.

An experience report requires different information for the program committee.

5.3.2 Information for an Experience Report

If you propose an experience report, the More Information box is your chance to describe your *story*.

You might consider a paragraph for each of these points:

1. Start with the problems, the initial state before your experience began. What kinds of problems did you see? You might have to add the number of teams or products involved.
2. What triggered the need for a change?
3. What did you try? What succeeded?
4. Did what you try make the problem worse? When did you make things better? What was *your* experience for each of these tries and fails? How did you feel? The more emotions you uncover, the better the experience report.

5. What did you and the organization learn as you proceeded with the tries and fails/successes?
6. What is the new, updated state?

Not all experience reports can report a positive change. Sometimes, everything the writer tried failed. Everyone can learn
from a failed attempt at change. Please do consider writing an
experience report about things that failed.

Experience reports are not just about the company's transfor-
mation. If you are the reporter, please write about how *you*
changed also. One of the reports I shepherded recently said
that the more vulnerable he felt, the better I liked the report.

I wasn't looking for vulnerability. I was looking for the kernel
of the experience. He delivered and it was a great report.

5.4 Always Explain the Story Behind the Session

In all the More Information boxes, I suggested you start with
a story to set the context. I'm talking about a few minutes for
a story that highlights the major problems your audience can
relate to. That story helps you connect with the audience.

An experience report is an entire story, so the starting story is
the beginning context.

A short story—not more than about 3-5 minutes—helps you
set the context for the entire session. If you can add a little
humor, that's great. (See Start With a Story for one example
of how I use a story to set the context for the session.)

I use sarcasm, eye-rolling, and a little self-deprecating humor.
Just enough so people realize I'm human.

Discover what works for you, first for the opening story and then throughout the rest of the session. Find the best version of your speaking self.

5.5 Explain When Your Ideas Won't Work

You have experience solving problems in a specific context. It's possible your solutions are universal. In my experience, a universal solution is almost never universal.

When you set the context and explain when your solutions might not work for the audience, you create more credibility than if you say your solution will work for everyone.

I often add these details in the More Information part of the proposal. I've used these approaches:

- Set aside five minutes somewhere in the outline to discuss when my suggestions won't work.
- Discuss anti-patterns or other problems as I proceed.
- If I think I'll run out of time in the session, write a blog post or article and refer to that content in the session.

Don't be afraid to say when your ideas won't work. Every time I've done this, people argue with me. I've heard this, "You said this wouldn't work in my context, but it does. You're wrong!"

That's the kind of wrong I like. I smile and thank the person.

5.6 Complete the Other Fields

You might see keywords, room setup, and more. Complete all those fields except for the bio and the title now. If you're not sure what any field is, ask someone on the program committee. Ask as early as you can, so you can finish the proposal early.

5.7 Refine Your Proposal

Open your proposal document so you can add all this information.

As you add these ideas to your proposal, you might realize you want to refine your original ideas.

Do refine the frame, including the people you want to attract to your session, the outcomes, and your abstract. Do not worry about making your audience too small. A few of the right people are much more valuable to you than too many of the wrong people.

1. Decide if and what kinds of interactions you want to offer. Then decide what session type you want to offer.
2. How well will that session type work for the problems your people want to solve?
3. Review the abstract and the outcomes. Can you deliver with this session type?
4. If you can't deliver with the session type you selected, do you need to change any outcomes?

Now, it's time to write a bio and add your speaking experience.

6. Write a Bio to Establish Your Expertise

Your bio establishes your expertise, authority, and credibility in your field. If your conference proposal has a speaking experience field, use that field to explain your expertise, authority, and credibility. I like to think of the bio and speaking experience fields as ways to connect with and invite the right people to your session:

- These fields help the program committee realize you know what you're talking about.
- These fields help the program committee say yes to you, based on your work and speaking experience.
- These fields help the potential audience realize your session is the one they must attend, out of the entire conference.

I want to be the reason people come to a conference. Am I always? Oh, no! But sometimes? Yes. Why do I want that? Because I know my sessions offer value to the right people. I want the right people to see my bio and say "Yes" to my session.

I am not talking about inflating your experience. Never do that. Be honest about your experience. I have some example bios below for people with a couple of years of experience.

Your bio and speaking experience fields help people realize how good you are at this aspect of your role and in your speaking.

6.1 Consider This Template for Your Bio

I iterate on my bio just like I iterate on everything else in a conference proposal. Many conferences ask for a 100-word bio. I have a "template" I use for my bio:

- Line 1: Introduce you, as a speaker, to the reader. Use verbs.
- Line 2: Help people see your expertise.
- Line 3: Add your credibility.
- Line 4: Other details that might help people see how your expertise relates to the potential audience.
- Line 5: Wow them with something, if you can. At a minimum, direct people to your site.

Here's my speaking bio, in specific lines, so you can see how I use that template:

1. Johanna, known as the Pragmatic Manager, offers frank advice for your product development challenges.
2. She works with individuals, teams, and leaders across the organization to resolve risks and see alternatives for their product development.
3. As a consultant, she's led hundreds of workshops, delivered talks and keynotes around the world, and dipped her toes into Pecha Kuchas.

4. She's the author of 17 books and counting.
5. She blogs on jrothman.com and createadaptablelife.com and writes columns around the web.

Here's how to dissect that bio: In Line 1, I use my first name because I want people to connect with *me*, as a human being. That's why I don't talk about my degrees, certifications, or other external institutional recognition.

Even if I held a PhD, I wouldn't use it in my bio. As for certifications, as I write this in 2020, the agile community has too many framework battles. I want to encourage people from the various framework camps to participate in my session, not push them away. I use my bio to connect with other people, not give them a reason to reject me.

Line 2 explains what I do. I use the word "works" because it's active and vague about what I do. I lead workshops; coach people and teams; consult with various people; speak; and create my own intellectual property. I don't use the "is" word anywhere in the bio. That's too passive for what I want the bio to do. You might lead, manage, create, facilitate, build, and more. Use verbs that convey action in your bio.

Line 3 conveys the breadth and depth of my speaking experience. If you work inside an organization, you may not have a similar level of speaking experience. In the examples below, I'll suggest how you might showcase your speaking skill.

Line 4 establishes my authority and expertise. I supposed I could have said "An award-winning author, Johanna has published 17 books and counting." However, this is a *speaking* bio, not a writing bio. The program committee needs to see I know my material. They don't need to know about everything I've written. Yet.

Line 5 directs people to my website. That's where they can discover more about me. Here are some example bios, specifically for non-consultants who don't have a ton of experience:

> Jill Jones, currently a technical lead for BigCloud-ServiceProvider, experiments with agile approaches in teams and across the organization. She's led several teams through their experiments with TDD, ATDD, and domain driven design. Along the way, she's learned about vanity metrics and metrics that work. She's a frequent organizer and participant in Chicago Lean Coffee and has spoken at a dozen meetups over the past two years.

Here's what's compelling to *me* about Jill's bio:

- The idea of "several teams through their experiments" with ideas and practices that are not common enough in our industry.
- I love the line about vanity metrics and metrics that work.
- Jill has built her speaking experience in several ways. Sure, Lean Coffee isn't precisely a talk or a workshop. However, it is facilitation. And the mention of the "organization?" That's code for "helping people accomplish a specific goal."

Jill doesn't have a website. If she did, or if she blogged or wrote articles somewhere, she would mention that last.

> Jack Jones, a tester-turned-product-owner at BigRegulatedCompany, works to bring the customers

and feature teams together. He's learned how to coach the technical people and the customers to work together effectively. He's also coached his managers into using flow metrics, not resource metrics. He's spoken internally at BigRegulatedCompany internal conferences and to internal teams across the country for the past three years, spreading what real agile approaches look like. In addition, he's spoken at several agile meetups in Chicago.

Here's what's compelling to *me* about Jack's bio:

- He has experience as a tester and a product owner.
- He has regulated industry experience.
- Working together? Oh my, I want to hear about that.
- The flow metrics? You had me at flow.
- His speaking experience is mostly internal, but "across the country" is quite promising.

You don't need a ton of speaking experience to create a compelling bio so the program committee can say yes.

6.2 Your Speaking Experience Helps the Committee Say Yes

As you iterate through your bio, be honest with yourself about your speaking experience. If you have never delivered a session before now, start with a local conference or a meetup. And, don't tell the program committee you've never spoken before. Everyone starts somewhere. Could you start with a large international conference? You can. I recommend any of these formats:

- An Experience Report
- A Lighting Talk
- A Pecha Kucha

In all three of these formats, you get to tell a story. The time for each session tends to be short—not more than 30 minutes.

Shorter sessions that include a story means the program committee isn't taking a huge risk when they accept you. You need to have a compelling story—and that's why you started with the people and their problems back in Frame the Proposal.

If you're new to speaking, I suggest you start with smaller audiences. You might start with local meetups or groups. Then, maybe regional conferences. You don't have to take years to build your speaking "resume" if you're willing to speak a lot.

As an example, when I started to speak, I spoke at several local meetups and also sent in proposals to smaller conferences. By the time the conferences accepted my proposals, I had spoken at a minimum of six or seven local meetups.

And, if you're sure that the program committee for a larger conference will take your compelling proposal for a talk or a workshop even if you don't have any speaking experience, go for it. I could be totally wrong.

6.3 Iterate on the Proposal and Where to Submit

I iterate on all pieces of the proposal all the time. I make the abstract and outcomes as compelling as I can make them for the people with the problems.

When I realize there's a whole other class of people with similar problems, I have a choice: create another abstract or use this one? I tend to narrow my focus, rather than broaden it, which means two proposals. I recommend you do the same.

And, I iterate on where to submit my proposals.

If I want to experiment with a new talk, I'll ask a local meetup if I can speak at a monthly meeting. You might also look for local conferences to practice your topic.

The more local the conference or the meetup, the more likely the program committee will accept you, assuming your proposal meets their needs. Once a larger conference accepts your proposal, you can use local meetups to practice. You'll gain feedback on your proposal (did it meet the promise of your abstract?), your bio, and your session.

6.4 Update Your Proposal with Your Bio

As I iterate on my bio, I add it to the proposal document.

I also create a separate document with my bio and add it as a separate file in my "Speaking" folder. I keep that folder on my hard drive and backed up in the cloud. You might decide to iterate over your bio the more you choose to speak.

If you decide to write articles you might need a slightly different bio that emphasizes your writing accomplishments. I have found that the more I write, the more people seek out my presentations. And, the more I speak, the more people want to read my work.

1. Write out the four or five lines of your bio. I encourage you to try my template, but you can use any approach as long as you highlight your expertise, authority, and credibility.
2. Write out your speaking experience.
3. Based on your expertise, authority, and credibility, what three conferences will you propose this session to? If you want to make a larger list, that's great. You need a minimum of three conferences or meetups.

You've got everything except the title now. It's time to explore titles.

7. Hook Your Reader with a Great Title

You might wonder why I don't start writing a proposal with a title. In my experience, a great title is something I need to ponder and experiment with. I do often start with a placeholder title.

When I developed this multitasking talk, I used this title:

> Stop the madness. End the multitasking.

That was a good title to help me form my thoughts. It might not be such a great title for inviting people into my session—either the program committee or the participants at the conference. Why? I'm too close to telling people they're stupid for not being able to stop multitasking.

And, I find that what I plan to say changes as I work through the pieces of the proposal.

7.1 Titles Invite and Connect

The title is the single most important piece of the proposal. That's because readers see the title first.

A great title will:

- Grab the reader's attention.

- Invite the reader to read the abstract.
- Connect with the reader in some way.
- Help the reader remember your session when they get to the conference.

That's a lot of work for a title for a conference talk. And, it's a lot of work for less than a dozen words.

I've heard speakers say the title should be like "clickbait." That doesn't fit for me.

Clickbait often uses hyperbole to get people to click on a link. Here are some examples:

- Cutest kitten!
- Groom can't believe what bride looks like...
- Take this quiz to see what character you are...

I don't want my conference proposals to sound like or look like clickbait. I want people to click on my title because they want the content. Not because they can't help themselves.

I select a title to help people identify with the problems I can help them solve.

7.2 Titles Help the Reader Identify with the Problems You Solve

Because you've identified the problems people have and who those people are, you're already partway to a title.

I separate the title into two parts:

1. Part 1: What problems do people want to solve?
2. Part 2: What will they get if they solve those problems?

My current title for the multitasking talk is only okay. The first part, "Stop the madness" doesn't say much about multitasking. My current second part, "End the multitasking" is still part of the problem people want to solve. I'm not saying anything about what people get if they solve the problem.

That said, "*Stop the madness. End the multitasking*" isn't horrible. It's okay. Let's see if we can make it better.

I use title analyzers to see how good—or bad—my title is.

7.3 Check Your Possible Titles with a Headline Analyzer

I use two headline analyzers to check my titles. There are many more, but I've had good results with these:

- Advanced Marketing Institute's Headline Analyzer
- CoSchedule Headline Analyzer

Advanced Marketing Institute checks the "Emotional Marketing Value (EMV)" of your words. Here's what they say on the results page:

> "... English language contains approximately 20% EMV words. And for comparison, most professional copywriters' headlines will have 30%-40% EMV Words in their headlines, while the most

gifted copywriters will have 50%-75% EMV words in headlines."[1]

CoSchedule looks for word balance between Common, Uncommon, Emotional, and Power words[2].

The two analyzers return different results. That means I look for a balance between both of the analyzers.

As long as you check your headline, I suspect it doesn't matter which headline analyzer you use.

7.4 Create a Table of Results

Because I often discover I don't *start* with great titles, I create a table to track my ideas.

Here are the results for "Stop the madness. End the multitasking":

- CoSchedule gave it a score of 66. Not bad.
- AmInstitute gave it a score of 33%, evenly split between Intellectual and Empathetic. Again, not bad.

I could stop there and have a pretty good title. However, I want to see my other options. I brainstorm between three and six more options before I start analyzing them. Here are the options I originally developed for the multitasking talk:

- Say Yes—or Say No? What to Do When Faced with the Impossible

---

[1]https://www.aminstitute.com/headline/
[2]https://coschedule.com/headline-analyzer

- Say No to More Work
- Visualize Your Work So You Can Say No
- Measure Your Costs of Multitasking and Learn to Say No
- Rationalize Your Work and Stop Multitasking
- Say No to Multitasking and Keep Your Job

As I checked these titles, I also added this possibility:

- Say No to Multitasking and Keep Your Job if You Want

And, here is the table that compares the scores:

Title Score Comparison

Title	CoSchedule Score	AmInstitute Score
Stop the madness. End the multitasking	66	33%, evenly Intellectual and Empathetic
Say Yes—or Say No? What to Do When Faced with the Impossible	62	25%, only Spiritual
Say No to More Work	49	20%, only Spiritual
Visualize Your Work So You Can Say No	66	12.5%, Spiritual
Measure Your Costs of Multitasking and Learn to Say No	62	30%, evenly distributed across Intellectual, Spiritual, Emotional
Rationalize Your Work and Stop Multitasking	64	33%, evenly Intellectual and Empathetic
Say No to Multitasking and Keep Your Job	62	50%, all Intellectual
Say No to Multitasking and Keep Your Job If You Want	67	54.55%, evenly distributed!

I have a clear winner, "Say No to Multitasking and Keep Your Job if You Want."

Was I surprised? Oh, yes. I thought some of the others were much better. I was wrong. And, I hadn't considered either of the "Say No to Multitasking ..." alternatives until I looked at the two parts of the title again.

You might consider what I do: as I see what the headline analyzers say, I generate more options. That's how I got to the winning title.

I often set a 25-minute timebox to generate and check titles. That's because I sometimes get lost generating titles and I want to finish the proposal.

If you keep trying to generate titles and you can't create a title with a good score, try these ideas:

- Use synonyms for the words you're currently using.
- Use CoSchedule's prompts for the various kind of words, especially the power and emotional words. I tend towards the intellectual words, which doesn't grab people.
- Contact a friend or colleague with this problem and ask this question, "What will you get if you solve this problem?"

I also take breaks and walk if I'm stuck.

7.5 Troubleshoot Your Titles

You generated a title. You love it. You're sure it's perfect. And, the headline analyzers don't like it.

Put that title into another document. Save and close that document. Yes, I'm telling you to save it somewhere else. That title is off-limits now.

When you talk to your friends or colleagues—or even when you deliver the session—you can ask people, "What do you think of that (off-limits) title for this session?"

If your friends and colleagues are like mine, they might actually say, "What were you thinking? I don't understand how that title links to what you're saying."

Keep those friends. That's valuable feedback.

And, you might find that the title you can't use might be a catch-phrase of some sort. One of my original titles for the multitasking talk was, "Multitasking: the fastest way to slow everything down." That's a *great* sentence for the presentation or the workshop. It's a *horrible* title. But, once people participate in my session, they can see why multitasking slows everything down.

7.6 Consider These Prompts

When I'm under pressure and I need to get a title fast, I've used these prompts:

- Some Number of Tips or Secrets to the problem people have. I try for an odd number.
- Mistakes to Avoid When...
- How to ...
- Some number of Laws. Again, try for an odd number, such as five.

Now, take another look at the problems people want to solve and what they will get if they solve those problems. How can you craft a title that might use Secrets, Tips, Mistakes, How to, Laws?

Titles are copywriting. The more you want to persuade people of something, the more it's worth your time to learn copywriting.

7.7 Complete Your Proposal

If you have trouble titling the way I do, consider creating a separate document or spreadsheet to track your title possibilities. Then, once you have a title that's at least good enough, add it to your proposal document.

1. Make sure you generate at least six titles before you settle on one of them.
2. Check the headline analyzer before you settle on a title.
3. Select your "best" title, based on the headline analyzers and what you think. Be wary of overruling the headline analyzers. Add the title to your document with all the information.

One reminder about titles: Perfect is the enemy of the good. I recommend you spend not more than 25 minutes generating a title. With any luck, the program committee will offer feedback if they don't like the title.

Now you've got everything ready. You know which conferences you want to submit to. It's time to be ready for feedback from the program committee.

8. Understand Conference Feedback

The conference will offer feedback about your proposal in several ways:

- Interim feedback about the proposal itself.
- Acceptance or rejection of your proposal.

If you submit a proposal to the large conferences, the program committee will offer feedback. With any luck, that feedback will help you hone your proposal and make it better.

I have received terrific feedback. I also received feedback where I realized no one on the program committee had any idea what I was saying.

Why? I was an invited speaker specifically for new and novel concepts in the field. No one on the program committee had any experience with these new and novel concepts.

The more you experiment with alternative ways of working, the less the program team might understand your proposal.

Don't worry about that. This is your chance to iterate on the abstract, on the outcomes, and add more information to the proposal. It's also a chance to decide again if you want to propose to *this* conference.

If the program committee doesn't understand your material, first check that you explained the material well. If you did, and they still don't understand, find another conference to propose your session.

Don't waste your time speaking to people who aren't interested in learning what you have to offer. Move on, to another conference or meetup.

You can't gain feedback if you submit your proposal late. Make sure you propose your session early.

8.1 Propose Your Session Early

The larger and more prestigious the conference, the more reviewers the conference has. Those conferences offer the most possibility for feedback.

Take that feedback. I always find it useful.

Famous Speakers Can Spook Reviewers

I often propose to some large, famous conferences. I propose my sessions as early as I can. And, sometimes, I wait and wait and wait for feedback.

I'm not shy, so I've queried the track chairs or the head of the program committee. I was quite surprised when one track chair told me some of the reviewers were intimidated by me. (I'm famous in my section of the world. Probably not in your section of the world.)

I am opinionated—as you can tell. And, I don't chew

people up and spit them out. I explained I really wanted feedback. I'm one of those stupid or brave people—I often propose new sessions for the large conferences.

When the track chair explained I wanted feedback just like everyone else, I got great feedback. I revamped that session and it succeeded. I've also received great feedback on titles.

You can't receive feedback if you don't propose early enough.

As an example, the Agile 20xx and the XP20xx conferences open submissions at least 8 months before the conference. The submissions remain open for anywhere from 6-12 weeks. (The actual dates vary year to year.)

If you propose your session in the first month, the reviewers will offer you substantive feedback.

The longer you wait to propose a session, the longer it will take for you to get feedback. And, the less feedback you will receive. That's because the reviewers have many more proposals to read and review.

If you wait until just before the submission system closes, you might not receive any feedback at all.

Don't wait until the last possible minute. This book is about preparing everything you need for your proposal in one proposal document. Armed with everything in one place, you can copy and paste the pieces into the online submission.

One note: as you copy and paste, make sure to review what the final proposal looks like. Make sure reviewers can read what you wrote. I've had to offer this feedback too often for proposals I need to read: "Please use carriage returns so I can read what you wrote."

Every submission system I've seen allows you to see what the proposal looks like. You can edit the proposal if it's not readable.

8.2 Respond to Feedback Fast

Every time I've received feedback, I try to respond within 24 hours. Even if I just say, "Thanks, you made me think!"

If you disagree with the feedback, ask for more information first.

I've received feedback where I was pretty sure the reviewer wanted me to deliver *his* talk. I asked him some questions about his context. I realized I'd missed a whole category of people with the same problem.

That's when I realized the reviewer was one of the people with the problems *and* he didn't understand what I had written. I has assumed too much expertise.

That was quite valuable feedback.

I did not assume my reviewer was stupid or ignorant or wrong. I received confirmation that he was part of my ideal audience *and* he needed more information.

I changed my outcomes, my abstract, and some of the "More" information. I showed how I started at Point A, moved through Point B, and onto Points C and D.

Because I brought the reviewers through my thinking and showed my thinking throughout the various parts of the proposal, the conference took my proposal. And, when I delivered the session, people thanked me for including what I originally thought was too "basic" information.

Without that reviewer's feedback, I would never have thought to include that "basic" information. Because I was so comfortable with these ideas, I'd lost track of what people thought was basic. I offered information that was not basic at all.

I've also received feedback on my titles. Before about 2017, my titles stunk. I only started to use this system of titling I described here in the past couple of years. Before then, I had a more random approach to titles. (Even now, I wonder about my titles.)

In every case where I received feedback for my titles, I've been able to create better titles.

I've proposed talks where the reviewers wanted workshops. I worry about workshops at some of the large conferences. My experience is that people want the recipe, not to have to think.

If I choose a workshop, I work hard at setting the context in the abstract and in the room. In the abstract, I say, "Bring something to write on, to develop your experiments," or some equivalent language.

In the session, before the session officially starts, I say, "This is a workshop. You're going to work here." I also use the word "Workshop" on the title slide. That helps.

You always have a choice with feedback. You don't have to take the feedback the reviewers offer. If you're lucky, several people will respond to your proposal and you can see what they all think.

At some point, you'll receive the conference decision. I assume you:

- Iterated on your proposal to make it the best writing you could.
- Proposed your session early.
- Responded to feedback.
- Where appropriate, you integrated that feedback into your proposal.

You did the best job you could on the proposal. Now, the conference will accept or reject your proposal. Not you. The proposal.

8.3 Manage Your Rejection

The large conferences reject many more proposals than they accept. They might even reject your fine proposal. The program committee rejected your proposal for any of these (or other) reasons:

- A more-famous person proposed a very similar session. The program committee accepted their proposal.
- The program had 45 proposals similar to yours. The program committee accepted one of those 45 proposals. Not yours.
- The conference has some limit on the number of proposals the program committee can accept from one person. They took one of your two proposals.
- The conference doesn't want that topic.

You can't do anything about these problems for now.

You can choose how you react.

8.4 Acknowledge Your Feelings

I don't know of a person who likes any kind of a rejection. I certainly don't like conference rejections.

Rejection *feels* personal to me. Intellectually, I know the program committee rejected my *proposal* and not *me*.

Just because I know that intellectually does not mean I can translate that knowledge to my emotions. I've had to learn that rejection was not about me. The rejection might not be about my ideas. Maybe the conference doesn't want that topic.

And, even if the program committee rejected my ideas, I am still a person of value. You, too.

I tend to take a contrarian stand in my proposals. I often propose something other than the "accepted" ways of thinking or acting.

Not all program committees like contrarians. Long ago, one program committee person told me, "You're a scary person to add to the conference. People either love you or hate you."

I said, "Isn't that a feature, not a defect?"

"No," he said. "If we add you to the program, we're endorsing your views and your perspectives. Our sponsors don't like the fact that you say there's no need for tools."

I found that an interesting perspective.

I never think a conference endorses the ideas of a given speaker. And, I was surprised the program committee thought a speaker might alienate the conference sponsors.

People—both the program committee and the sponsors—might play politics with the speakers. I can't do anything about that. The one thing I can do is to create the best proposal I can create.

If you receive a rejection, do ask why. You might ask a specific reviewer. You might ask the program committee chair or someone else in the program committee hierarchy. Here are ways I've asked for feedback:

- Is there something that would have made you say, "Yes" to my proposal?
- Is there something in the proposal that made you say, "No" to my proposal?
- I sometimes ask, "Can you explain why you didn't accept my proposal?"

You might not receive an answer. However, when the program committee rejects my proposal, I want to understand why. I then have the option to change what I do in the future.

8.5 Manage the Acceptance

The conference accepted your proposal. Wonderful! Congratulations!

Now, you still have some decisions to make. Read the contract the conference offers you. With any luck, the contract won't be longer than about a page in length. And, the contract explains the terms and conditions in language you can read.

I am not a lawyer. This is not legal advice.

I am a speaker and consultant who has seen more than her fair share of crazy contracts for a conference talk or workshop.

If you can't read the language, ask for an explanation of each clause. Remember, a contract is a whole document. If one clause negates another, you can ask to strike both clauses or rewrite one or both.

Sometimes, the conference will say, "This is our standard contract." You're not a standard person. You have a choice about whether to accept this contract. If you sign the contract, you accept the terms and conditions.

Do you want to accept the conference's terms and conditions?

Here are some terms and conditions that have made me rethink particular conferences:

1. The conference wants to own my presentation. Yes, they want the copyright to my slides. However, my copyright has value to me.
2. The conference wants to record me (audio and video) for reuse later. They don't want to pay me for that or to give me a copy. Any recordings have value to me.
3. I need to pay to participate in the conference. If I'm presenting at a session, I have invested much more than the conference fee.

You might have other reasons to say yes or no. Let me explain my concerns.

8.5.1 Your Copyright has Value

I am still not a lawyer. This is not legal advice.

I own my intellectual property. I sometimes write for hire, where I do not own my copyright. However, other than writing, I own all my presentations. I own my books.

I never give copyright to my slides. I recommend you do not either.

When you relinquish copyright, you relinquish your rights to the form of the content. If you use words on a slide in some way, you relinquish your right to use those words again, in that form.

That means you can't use those words in a book. Or an article. Or in anything that would offer you more visibility later. Those words are no longer yours.

Any conference that asks for your copyright probably has many more lawyers than you do. Even if you think you've done nothing wrong later, do you really want to fight with them?

I first check with my conference contact. Often, the people who organize the conference are at the mercy of their lawyers. They don't realize what the copyright clause means.

If they are not willing to change my contract with the conference, I politely decline to sign the contract. I often say, "I'm disappointed I won't be able to participate in the conference. However, I will not assign my copyright to you."

When they say, "We would never stop you from using your own words," I repeat my disappointment and repeat my lack of participation.

Some of these conferences have offered me a personal conference contract that is different from the other speakers. Under those conditions, I have accepted the contract.

8.5.2 Audio and Video Recordings Offer Value

When the conference wants to record you for posterity, what value does that recording have for them?

For example, the Agile conferences offers some of the conference videos on their site for free to entice future conference attendees. They put some of the videos behind a members-only wall, as value for the members.

What will the conference do with the video or audio? And, can you also record the audio without violating the contract?

Recordings offer me value, too.

I often record my presentations on my phone. When I listen to the recording later, I note what I could have said better, or how I said it. I have used these various recordings to improve.

Here are the conditions I've added to the contract to make the value work for both the conference and me:

- I receive a high definition digital copy of that recording in all forms.
- The conference does not make money off future viewings of that audio or video.
- If the conference wants to have people pay for the audio or video in the future, I negotiate a separate fee with the conference for their ability to do so.

When I speak at a conference, I assume I am speaking once. Not for the foreseeable future.

8.5.3 Conference Fees Offer Value

A conference once asked me to keynote their conference. While they were willing to pay an honorarium, they wanted me to pay to participate in the conference.

I asked them why they wanted me to pay. (I was curious.)

They said, "Everyone except the conference committee pays."

I asked how many people were on the conference committee. 60. How many speakers? 20.

I suggested they could slim their conference committee and offer registration to speakers. They didn't like that suggestion. I declined their invitation.

I do not understand any conference that wants speakers to pay to participate. Speakers, like the people on the conference committee, spend significant preparation time to create a great proposal and then a great session.

If the conference doesn't make enough money to pay for a speaker's registration, do you want to speak there?

8.6 Verify Conference Logistics

Part of managing your acceptance to a conference is to verify the conference logistics.

When you start to think about proposing a session for a conference, I recommend you Decide Which Conferences to Select.

Even if you had selection criteria, things sometimes change. Here's where I verify the logistics for the session and the conference:

- Will they pay my travel expenses?
- Is there an honorarium for the session?
- What deliverables do they expect?
- While I'm there, can I offer to do another session of some sort? This is where I might offer a Lightning Talk or a Pecha Kucha.

Let's discuss deliverables. I don't use PowerPoint. Some people love it. I don't. I use Keynote for my presentations.

You have many choices for how to organize your session. You don't need PowerPoint or Keynote. Some of my colleagues use Prezi. Some colleagues who want to incorporate polls throughout their presentations use web-based apps that incorporate polls. Some colleagues draw their presentation as they proceed.

You don't need presentation software to deliver a terrific session.

As of this year, I have stopped accepting invitations to speak if the conference wants a PowerPoint file of my talk. I'm happy to offer a pdf. I won't offer PowerPoint.

Some conferences want to offer me feedback on my slides. I always take the offer of feedback. However, I have received feedback that says, "No speaker notes. We can't tell what she's going to say."

Of course you can't tell what I'm going to say. I use slides as a way to organize the sequence of my thoughts and stories. I'm going to talk to people at the conference and adjust what I say *in the moment*. That's why we offer talks and we don't read our slides to the audience.

I also don't use a conference's "template." Too often, the templates I've seen had difficult-to-read fonts, or fonts that don't render correctly on my machine. In addition, the templates too often assume a speaker has only text on the slide. There's no room for images. Worse, the organizers didn't create a real template. Instead they stuffed a file full of images so the file was too large to send.

Conferences who want to "brand" all sessions with the same template show me they don't understand branding. I won't propose a session for those conferences. Or, I won't accept their terms when they tell me the terms.

You might not be as picky as I am. And, I might reconsider whether I want to participate in the conference when I see the terms.

Only you can generate your criteria for conferences. Make sure you do have criteria so you can manage your acceptance.

8.7 How Much is the Honorarium?

An honorarium is some form of compensation for your presentation. I've already discussed travel expenses and the conference registration. I have a list of my choices in Decide Which Conferences to Select.

You can always speak for "free." Assuming the conference does some form of marketing, you will receive exposure from their promotion efforts. Those efforts offer you some value. If you are a new speaker, this might fit for you.

I almost always speak for free when I don't have to travel. I speak at local meetups anywhere in the world if I'm already there. I enjoy speaking and I like meeting new people. I offer to speak in the form of one-hour talk and a question and answer period. (If the organizers want something more than an evening meetup, I negotiate other terms.)

For conferences, I expect some form of honorarium. I expect something for a one-hour (or so) session. I expect more for a keynote or a longer workshop.

You will have to decide what you want. For years, I spoke for minimal honoraria at conferences. I even led a half-day tutorial once for no compensation when I was a brand new speaker. I didn't realize I should have asked for money for that longer session.

The honorarium is almost never enough to cover the cost of the time you spend in preparation for the session. However, the honorarium helps when you ask yourself, "Is this conference worth it for me?"

However, I recommend you ask the question when you verify the logistics."How much is the honorarium?" helps you and the conference realize you offer substantial value.

8.8 Write This Down

I use a different document to write down my conference criteria. That way, if someone calls me, I can open the document and ask coherent questions. Create a document so you write these criteria down:

1. When can you propose a session for maximum feedback?
2. When can you expect an accept/reject decision?
3. If the conference rejects your proposal, who can you ask for more information?

4. What criteria will allow you to accept a conference's offer to present a session?
   - Do you need travel expenses?
   - Do you need a specific honorarium?
   - Do you need anything else to make this a win-win for everyone?

Now that you're thinking about accepting a conference's invitation to present your session, let's circle back to why you should consider speaking. Ask the questions every potential speaker can ask.

9. Consider Speaking at a Conference

All through this book, I've assumed you want to speak at a conference. You have expertise to share, or an experience to report.

Or, you might be a consultant, as I am, and you want to market yourself through speaking.

Here's another reason to speak at a conference: When you write or speak, you reinforce your knowledge. I learn when I don't know about a topic in detail—I call this handwaving—*and* when I have deep knowledge about that topic.

When I write proposals, I see more possibilities—for me, for my clients, and for people who might have a different context. I *learn* from writing the proposal.

9.1 Why Propose a Session?

I meet too many people who say, "I'm not a professional speaker. I'm just a 'something' kind of person."

You are not "just a something." You have experience that will help someone in a certain context.

You can choose to learn to be a professional speaker. That is, professional in your approach, professional in how you create a session, and how you deliver that session.

Sometimes, people tell me they feel as if they are imposters when they propose a session.

You are not an imposter. Far from it.

I have learned these valuable lessons when I propose a session:

- Is my experience unique? Or, is it applicable to more contexts?
- Does my experience help people understand what they should try to avoid?
- I gain feedback about the session content.
- I learn more about how to explain my reasoning from the program committee's comments about the session.

Ask yourself these questions, before and after you propose a session. When you answer these questions, you will recognize you do not have Impostor Syndrome.

Recognize Impostor Syndrome

The less experience we have with something, such as proposing or delivering a session, the more we might feel as if we are frauds. That's Impostor Syndrome.

The more you feel as if you are a fraud or an impostor, the less you think you have something valuable to say.

I can't tell you *how* to feel. I advise you to ask yourself the questions I suggested above, to see if you can use what you learn from the feedback on the session. Assess your experience. Decide if the session type will work for the experience you have.

Remember, you are the only one who knows your experience, your story. How will your story offer value to other

> people?

When I work through a session proposal, I always learn something.

9.2 Why Speak at a Conference?

The more I speak, the more I learn what I know and don't know. I learn the edges of my experience, which helps me decide which kinds of experience I want to gain.

- I learn when I create the abstract.
- I learn when I create the session.
- I learn from the program commitee's comments and feedback.
- I learn from the audience questions.

I even learn when the conference rejects my proposal. Back in 2012, I proposed a job search session to the Agile conference based on my job search book. The conference rejected my proposal. However, the feedback I received on the proposal allowed me to deliver that short workshop many times since 2012. The feedback was invaluable.

And, since I'm an extrovert—which means I speak in order to think—I learn what I think when I speak.

Introverts learn in their heads before they speak. I recognize this although I don't understand it.

Conference speaking offers everyone these benefits:

- You learn how to frame your ideas in ways other people can understand.
- You gain the feedback to push you into more ways of learning.
- You gain a larger network of people with whom you can engage in further learning.

Every time you speak, you invite people into your network. I learn when these people ask me questions or discuss my ideas.

I have benefited from almost every session I've led. Even the sessions where I spoke to "only" five people. That session led to several consulting engagements and even more learning.

The only time I have not benefited directly from a session is when the conference didn't attract my kind of audience. I learned about that type of conference and to stay away from similarly framed future conferences.

9.3 Decide Which Conferences to Select

You might wonder, "How can I choose which conferences to propose a session for?" I suggest you create criteria for yourself for the conferences.

As you've seen, preparing a proposal, never mind the session prep and delivery, takes time. I make decisions to speak based on what's going on in my business, and the various Costs of Delay I might incur by taking time for a conference.

9.3.1 Use Context-Free Questions

I know that I will write and speak about what I want to be known for over the course of a year. I know I will create on-site and virtual workshops. I know I will speak, coach, consult.

The question is how much of each?

Here are two closed questions I ask when I receive a speaking request:

- Am I available?
- Is the request far enough in advance that I can manage the request?

Assuming I am available and I can manage this request, I can now ask context-free questions:

- Is this topic something I want to be known for?
- Do I or will I enjoy speaking about this topic?
- What will I gain from participating?
- What will I lose from participating?

These are context-free questions. Note that they apply to any speaking request.

Here's an example. A conference that required international travel asked me to speak as a track talk about 45 days in advance. They paid coach airfare and my hotel room for the entire conference because it was a track talk. No hotel reimbursement before or after the two days of the conference. I would have needed more than 15 hours of travel to manage the request.

I'm not offended by a track talk. More of "my" people come to a track talk. I would rather speak to 10 engaged potential clients than 5000 unengaged people who feel trapped at a keynote.

I said, *No*. The organizer asked, *Why not?* I explained I would need to arrive early to manage my jet lag. I also said that to cross an ocean, I require business class airfare. (Business class is about sleeping. It has nothing to do with food or drink. I rarely eat when flying east to Europe. Flying west is often different and depends on where I start.)

Because they didn't reimburse business airfare and more hotel nights, I couldn't afford the hit to my business.

Now, that's an international request. I might think differently about a domestic request.

When I speak for a domestic audience, I still use my questions. I speak at conferences to explore new ideas and gain clients. I do see my speaking as marketing. Then, I ask this question about what I will lose from participating:

> *How much will it cost me to speak at this conference?*

I have a number of out-of-pocket costs: transportation to/from the airport both ways, airfare, hotel nights, food.

Notice that I didn't count the conference registration. I expect conference registration. I think of the conference registration as part of my honorarium. That part helps me fully participate in the conference.

There is also the cost to my business—the opportunity costs to my business. When I'm at a conference, I'm conferring. I'm not writing. I'm not creating or delivering workshops. I'm not coaching or consulting. I'm at the conference.

If you go to enough conferences, you've seen consultants fly in, give their talk, and fly out. They don't stay to talk with others and learn from other sessions. The honorarium isn't enough. If they remained at the conference, they would lose money in their business. It doesn't make sense to stay at the conference.

You will need to assess the honorarium for yourself.

9.3.2 Assess the Honorarium

As I suggested in How Much is the Honorarium?, I recommend you consider the honorarium when you decide which conferences to select for your speaking.

As an example, here are *my* honorarium criteria for selecting a conference:

- The conference has to want proposals about agile approaches.
- The conference will pay all of my airfare. For *me*, this is business class across an ocean. You will have to decide what fits for you. (I often pay my airport transfers myself. If the conference is paying for airfare, I'm happy to pay for the taxi or limo to and from the hotel.)
- Hotel rooms, including before and after the conference, especially if the conference is near a weekend. (When conference organizers negotiate hotel contracts, those extra nights pay for themselves in lower conference room rental or food and beverage costs.)

- An honorarium. This doesn't have to be money, although I prefer money. Some conferences buy one of my books for everyone who registers. I've conducted private sessions with local managers, a one-day pre-conference or post-conference workshop. When you consider your need for an honorarium, make it a win-win for the conference.

Notice that I didn't say I wanted any of these perks:

- A speaker tour for out-of-country speakers. I love tours. I once accepted a tour that lasted from 8 a.m. on Sunday until 8 p.m. on Sunday. We were supposed to have dinner after the tour. I had soup in my room because I was speaking at 8:30 a.m. on Monday. I need enough sleep before I speak.
- A speaker dinner during the conference or before the conference starts. I have had to leave speaker dinners at 9 pm without having been served because I was the keynote speaker at 8:30 am and I need my sleep. (I travel with meal replacement bars because this occurs way too often.) I like spending time with the conference committee. And, I want to speak when I'm refreshed and awake.
- "All meals." Even before I started to low-carb, I wanted protein at breakfast and lunch. Especially in the U.S., breakfast is all carbs with no protein or fat. Speakers cannot afford an insulin high that falls to rock-bottom just before they speak.

I need to take care of myself in order to speak well. You do, too.

And, if you're wondering about the limo to or from an airport? I seek fixed-price limos with air conditioning in the summer and heat in the winter. Those rides tend to be less expensive than a taxi or ride-sharing service at the airport.

Some speakers want to make sure there is gender parity for the speakers. That's not one of my goals. I expect I will be such a great speaker that the conference committee will ask themselves why they don't have more women. And, while I'm there, I have no trouble asking questions about the diversity of speakers.

I have some criteria that eliminate some conferences for me:

- Conferences where I compete with other speakers for a limited travel budget. I don't believe in zero-sum games and won't play them.
- When the program committee tells me I'll get "exposure" instead of travel expenses and an honorarium. I'm already exposed. I don't need a conference to expose me more.
- I never pay to speak at a conference.

These are my criteria, not yours. I strongly recommend you consider what would make you say *yes* to a conference and what would make you say *no*. The more you know what you want, the easier it is to decide which conferences to submit to, and what would make you say *yes*.

9.4 Prepare in Advance for Conferences

I recommend you write all these ideas down somewhere in a master file. When I review my yearly plan, I can see which conferences fit and don't fit.

1. Review the dates for your selected conferences. How early can you submit your proposal? Mark the dates on your calendar. You can always decide to not submit a proposal. However, if you're not aware of the dates, you can't propose a session.
2. Submit your proposal on the first possible date. Make sure you receive a confirmation email. Investigate if you do not receive a confirmation email.
3. Iterate on everything to do with the conference proposal, including feedback.

I wish you the best in your speaking endeavors. If you've done all the writing as we proceeded, toast yourself with a beverage of your choice.

I hope this book is valuable to you. If it was, do let me know how.

10. More from Johanna

People know me as the "Pragmatic Manager." I help leaders and teams see simple and reasonable alternatives that might work in their context—often with a bit of humor. Equipped with that knowledge, they can decide how to adapt how they work.

See www.jrothman.com for my blogs and other writing.

If you liked this book, you might also like the other nonfiction books I've written:

Management Books:

- *Practical Ways to Manage Yourself: Modern Management Made Easy, Book 1*
- *Practical Ways to Lead and Serve—Manage—Others: Modern Management Made Easy, Book 2*
- *Practical Ways to Lead an Innovative Organization: Modern Management Made Easy, Book 3*
- *Behind Closed Doors: Secrets of Great Management*
- *Hiring Geeks That Fit*

Product Development:

- *From Chaos to Successful Distributed Agile Teams: Collaborate to Deliver*
- *Create Your Successful Agile Project: Collaborate, Measure, Estimate, Deliver*

- *Manage Your Project Portfolio: Increase Your Capacity and Finish More Projects, 2nd ed*
- *Agile and Lean Program Management: Scaling Collaboration Across the Organization*
- *Diving for Hidden Treasures: Uncovering the Cost of Delay Your Project Portfolio*
- *Predicting the Unpredictable: Pragmatic Approaches to Estimating Project Cost or Schedule*
- *Project Portfolio Tips: Twelve Ideas for Focusing on the Work You Need to Start & Finish*
- *Manage It!: Your Guide to Modern, Pragmatic Project Management*

Personal Development:

- *Free Your Inner Nonfiction Writer*
- *Become a Successful Independent Consultant*
- *Write a Conference Proposal*
- *Manage Your Job Search*

I'd like to stay in touch with you. If you don't already subscribe, please sign up for my email newsletter, the Pragmatic Manager. Please connect with me on LinkedIn, or follow me on Twitter, @johannarothman.

Did this book help you? If so, please consider writing a review of it. Reviews help other readers find books. Thanks!

Johanna

www.ingramcontent.com/pod-product-compliance
Lightning Source LLC
Chambersburg PA
CBHW060254030426
42335CB00014B/1697